Compiled by the Editors
Designed and Illustrated

W9-BCP-782

an imprint of
■ SCHOLASTIC
www.scholastic.com

Copyright © 2005 Scholastic Inc.

Scholastic and Tangerine Press and associated logos are trademards of Scholastic Inc.
Published by Tangerine Press, an imprint of Scholastic Inc; 557 Broadway, New York, NY 10012

10 9 8 7 6 5 4 3 2 1

ISBN: 0-439-85098-3

Printed and bound in Canada

Warning:

Humor may be hazardous to your bad mood!

Side Splitters

What's a baby's motto?
**If first you don't succeed—
cry, cry again!**

Which detective takes
bubble baths?
Sherlock Foams.

What did one toe say to the other?
**"Don't look now, but there are a
couple of heels following us!"**

3

Why do only small elves
live under toadstools?
**Because there is
not mushroom.**

Who earns a living driving
their customers away?
A taxi driver.

Where do pianists
go for vacation?
Florida Keys.

I don't have lungs or a chest but I need air. I am not alive, but I grow. I don't have a mouth, and I'm allergic to water. What am I?

Answer: Fire.

I run but I never walk. I have a mouth but I never talk. I have a bed but I never lie. What am I?

Answer: A river.

Actress: Have you ever
seen me on T.V.?
Fan: On and off.
Actress: How did you like me?
Fan: Off.

Did you hear about
the actor who fell
through the floor?
**It was just a
stage he was
going through.**

Beth: Would you remember me in an hour?

John: Sure.

Beth: Would you remember me in a minute?

John: Sure.

Beth: Would you remember me in a second?

John: Sure.

Beth: Knock, Knock

John: Who's there?

Beth: You forgot me already!

You're a bus driver. At the first stop, 4 people board the bus. At the second stop, 8 people board. At the third stop, 2 people get off and at the forth stop, everyone gets off. The question is... what color are the bus driver's eyes?

Answer: The same as yours because you're the bus driver!

David's father has three sons :
Snap, Crackle, and _____ ?

Answer: David!

Why did the atoms
cross the road?
It was time to split.

Why do bagpipers walk
when they play?
**They're trying to get
away from the noise.**

Why shouldn't you give
someone a gate?
**Because they might
take afence.**

What has three feet and can't walk?
A yard stick.

What has two legs
but can't walk?
A pair of pants.

What kind of ears
do trains have?
Engineers.

What kind of teeth
cost one dollar?
Buck teeth.

What gets wetter
the more it dries?
A towel.

What building has
the most stories?
The library.

What kind of truck
gets the hiccups?
A hiccup truck.

What time is the best time
to go to the dentist?
Tooth-hirty.

Why is the tooth
fairy so smart?
**She has a lot
of wisdom teeth.**

Why did the computer
have a back ache?
Because it slipped a disk.

How do wealthy
people dance?
Check-to-check.

Why did the man dance
in front of the bottle?
It said, "Twist to open."

Why did King Kong climb the
Empire State Building?
**Because he couldn't fit
in the elevator.**

What do you call
a fly without wings?
A walk.

How do you find King Arthur
in the dark?
With a knight light.

How does the barber do
his work so fast?
With short cuts.

How is an
engaged woman
like a telephone?
**They both
have rings.**

What did King Tut
say when he got scared?
"I want my mummy."

What did the dentist give
the marching band?
A tuba toothpaste.

What did the farmer say
when he lost his tractor?
"Where's my tractor?"

What did the judge
say to the dentist?
**"Do you swear to pull the tooth
and nothing but the tooth?"**

What did the lawyer
name his daughter?
Sue.

What did the mountain
climber name his son?
Cliff.

What did the policeman
say to his belly?
"You're under a vest."

What do lawyers wear to court?
Lawsuits.

What do tourists use to
get around the beach?
Taxi crabs.

What do you call a boy
with one foot in the door?
Just-in.

What do you call
a flying policeman?
A helicopper.

What do you call a giant
with lemons in his ears?
**Anything you want—
he can't hear you.**

What do you call a policeman
who never gets out of bed?
An undercover cop.

What do you get when
you mix your dad's red
paint with his white paint?
You get in trouble.

What goes up but
never comes down?
Your age.

What is a pirate's
favorite country?
Arrrrrrrgentina.

What kind of car
does an electrician drive?
A Volts-wagon.

What kind of jokes
did Einstein make?
Wisecracks.

What kind of soap does
a judge use?
"Trial" size soap.

What's the difference
between a jeweler and a jailer?
**The jeweler sells watches
and the jailer watches cells.**

What's a pirate movie rated?
Arrgh.

Which superhero travels by
public transportation?
Bus Lightyear.

Why are hairdressers
fast drivers?
**Because they know
all the shortcuts.**

Why are movie stars so cool?
Because they have many fans.

Why are opera singers
good sailors?
**Because they know how
to handle the high seas.**

Why couldn't the piano
teacher open the door?
He forgot his piano keys.

Why couldn't the
pirates play cards?
**Because the captain
was standing on the deck.**

Why did the doctor
lose his temper?
**Because he didn't
have any patients.**

Why did the king
draw straight lines?
Because he was the ruler.

Why did the king
go to the dentist?
To get his teeth crowned.

Why did the lady go outside
with her purse open?
**She expected change
in the weather.**

Why did the lumberjack
get mad at the computer?
Because he couldn't get logged on.

Why did the man
run around his bed?
**Because he wanted to
catch up on his sleep.**

Why did the princess go
to the print shop?
**So that she could find
her prints charming.**

Why did the
robber take
a bath?
**To make a clean
getaway.**

Why did the robber
wear blue gloves?
**Because he didn't want
to get caught red-handed.**

Why is the Queen's
bedroom flooded?
**Because she's reigned
for 50 years.**

Why was the fisherman
mad at the computer?
**Because he wasn't
getting any bytes.**

Why was the
scientist's head wet?
**Because he had
a brainstorm.**

Why would Snow White
make a good judge?
**Because she's the fairest
in the land.**

How do you unlock
a haunted house?
With a skeleton key.

Why did the skeleton
cross the road?
To get to the body shop.

What kind of horse
only comes out at Halloween?
A nightmare.

How do you make
a skeleton laugh?
Tickle its funny bone.

What do you call a skeleton
that won't get out of bed?
Lazy bones.

What do you call a mom who eats cookies in bed?

A crumb-y mummy.

How many witches does
it take to change a light bulb?
**Just one, but she changes it
into a frog.**

What do you call
two witches who
live together?
Broommates.

What happens when
you cross a witch and a clown?
A brew ha-ha.

What's a witch's
favorite computer program?
The spell checker.

What's the problem
with twin witches?
**You can never tell
which witch is which.**

Who lives in a sand castle?
A sand witch.

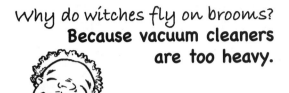

Why do witches fly on brooms?
Because vacuum cleaners are too heavy.

Funny Farm

Why was the sheep
pulled over on the highway?
It made an illegal ewe turn.

What do bees do
with their honey?
They cell it.

What do you get
when you cross
a bank with a skunk?
Dollars and scents.

What kind of banks do alligators use?
River banks.

Who always goes to bed with shoes on?
A horse.

What do you get when you cross
a werewolf with an octopus?
A fur coat with a lot of sleeves.

What is a kangaroo's favorite year?
Leap year.

How much money does a skunk have?
One scent.

What do bunnies
say on January 1?
Hoppy New Year.

41

What's black and white
and eats like a horse?
A zebra.

What did the judge say when the skunk
walked in the court room?
"Odor in the court."

Why do male deer need braces?
Because they have "buck teeth."

What happens when frogs park illegally?
They get toad.

What is green and jumps a lot?
A frog with hiccups.

What did the porcupine
say to the cactus?
"Is that you, Mommy?"

How do you catch a squirrel?
**Climb up a tree and
act like a nut.**

How did the starfish pay for his burger?
With a sand dollar.

How do porcupines play leapfrog?
Very carefully.

Why do fish live in salt water?
**Because pepper makes
them sneeze.**

Why are giraffes so slow to apologize?
**It takes them a long time
to swallow their pride.**

Why are skunks so smart?
Because they have a lot of scents.

Where do cows go
for vacation?
Moo York.

Why didn't the skunk
call his parents?
**Because his phone
was out of odor.**

What do penguins use for napkins?
Flapkins.

Where do killer whales go
to get braces?
The orca-dontist.

Why did the bunny cross the road?
**Because he wanted to show his
friends he could "hip hop."**

Did you hear about the fight
in the fish shop last night?
Two fish got battered.

What is crunchy, goes well with
milk, and goes "eek, eek, eek"
when you eat it?
Mice Krispies.

What is small, furry, and
great at sword fights?
A mouseketeer.

What do you get if you try to
cross a mouse with a skunk?
Dirty looks from the mouse.

What did Tom get when he
locked Jerry in the freezer?
Mice cubes.

What squeaks as it solves crimes?
Miami mice.

What is grey, has four legs and a trunk?
A mouse going to summer camp.

What's grey, squeaky, and
hangs around in caves?
Stalagmice.

What mouse was a Roman emperor?
Julius Cheeser.

Who is king of all the mice?
Mouse Tse Tung.

What do angry rodents send
each other at Christmas time?
Cross mouse cards.

What's the hardest part
of milking a mouse?
Getting it to fit over a bucket.

Hickory hickory dock.
The mouse ran up the clock.
The clock struck one,
**But the rest got away
with minor injuries!**

What do mice do when
they're at home?
Mousework.

What have 12 legs, six eyes,
three tails and can't see?
Three blind mice.

What is small, furry,
and smells like bacon?
A hamster.

When should a mouse
carry an umbrella?
**When it's raining
cats and dogs.**

What's the definition of
a narrow squeak?
A thin mouse.

Is there a mouse in the house?
**No, but there's a moose
on the loose.**

How do pigs write
top secret messages?
With invisible oink.

What do you call a pig
that does karate?
Porkchop.

What happened to the pig
that lost its voice?
It became disgruntled.

What happened when
the pig pen broke?
The pigs had to use a pencil.

How does a pig
go to hospital?
In a hambulance.

What do you get
when you cross
a pig with a dinosaur?
A Porkasaurus rex.

Why did it take the pig
hours to cross the road?
Because he was a slow-pork.

Why did the farmer call his pig "ink?" **Because it always ran out of the pen.**

Why should you never tell a pig a secret?
Because they love to squeal.

Where do farmers leave their
pigs when they go into town?
At porking meters.

What does a police officer use
when he arrests a pig?
Ham cuffs.

What do you get when you cross a grandmother and an octopus?
I don't know, but it sure can play Bingo.

What did one hammer say to the other hammer?
"I broke a nail."

Why was there thunder and lightning in the lab?
The scientists were brainstorming.

What did the dentist say to his computer?
"You have a severe megabyte."

What did one candle say to the other candle?
"Let's go out tonight."

What goes all around a pasture but never moves?

A fence.

**What did one firecracker say
to the other firecracker?**
"My pop's bigger than your pop."

How many feet are in a yard?
It depends on how many
people are standing in it.

**What kind of flower
grows on your face?**
Tulips.

**What kind of pants
does a ghost wear?**
Boo jeans.

**Why are monsters
such bad dancers?**
Because they have
seven left feet.

What do vampires wear in the fall?
Their bat-to-school clothes.

**How can you tell a martian
would be a good gardener?**
They all have green thumbs.

**What is a vampire's
favorite kind of coffee?**
De-coffin-ated.

**What did one ghost
say to the other?**
"Don't spook until
you're spooken to."

**How many sides
does a house have?**
Two: inside and outside.

How do you make a witch scratch?
Take away the W.

What two letters of the alphabet contain nothing?
MT.

What is the center of gravity?
The letter V.

What letter is found in a cup?
T.

How much dirt is in a hole 1 foot wide, 1 foot long, and 1 foot deep?
None—there is no dirt in a hole.

What occurs four times in every week, two times in every month, and once in a year?
The letter E.

If two is company, and three's a crowd— what are four and five?
Nine.

**What did one volcano
say to the other?**
"Do you lava me
like I lava you?"

**Three people were standing under
an umbrella...which one got wet?**
None of them, it wasn't raining.

**What did the sea
say to the sand?**
Nothing, it just waved.

Did you hear about the robbery last night?
Two clothespins held up a pair of pants.

What did one knife say to the other knife?
"You're looking pretty sharp today."

What has two hands, a big round face, always runs but stays in place?

A clock.

Why don't oysters give to charity?
Because they're shellfish.

**How can you get
four suits for a dollar?**
Buy a deck of cards.

**What do you get when you
cross a stream and a brook?**
Wet feet.

Why can't the magician tell his magic secrets in the garden?
The corn has ears, and the potatoes have eyes.

What do you get when you cross a bat and a bell?
A dingbat.

What kind of bean doesn't grow in a garden?
A human bean.

Why did the poor dog
chase his own tail?
**He was trying to make
both ends meet.**

Why do dogs wag their tails?
**Because no one else
will do it for them.**

What is a dog's favorite city?
New Yorkie.

How can you tell if
you have a dumb dog?
It chases parked cars.

What do dogs have that
no other animal has?
Puppy dogs.

Why did the Dachshund
bite the woman's ankle?
**Because he couldn't
reach any higher.**

What bone will a dog never eat?
A trombone.

What should you do
if your dog is missing?
Check the lost and hound.

What do you get if you
cross a giraffe with a dog?
**An animal that barks
at low flying aircraft.**

When is the most likely
time that a stray dog will
walk into your house?
When the door is open.

What did the cowboy say
when the bear ate Lassie?
"Well, doggone."

What is a dog's favorite sport?
Formula I drooling!

Where does a Rottweiler
sit at the movies?
Anywhere it wants to!

What is the best time to
take a Rottweiler for a walk?
Any time it wants to!

What do you get if you cross
a dog and a cheetah?
**A dog that chases cars -
and catches them.**

What happens when it rains cats and dogs?
You can step in a poodle.

What sort of clothes does a pet dog wear?
A petticoat.

What's a dog favorite hobby?
Collecting fleas.

What do you get if you cross
a dog with a blind mole?
**A dog that keeps barking
up the wrong tree.**

What dog loves to
take bubble baths?
A shampoodle.

How do you catch a runaway dog?
Hide behind a tree and make a noise like a bone.

What kind of dog sniffs out new flowers?
A bud hound.

Why is it called a "litter" of puppies?
Because they mess up the whole house.

How do you stop
a dog from smelling?
Plug its nose.

Why shouldn't you put an ad
in the paper if your dog is lost?
Because dogs can't read.

When is a black dog
not a black dog?
When it's a Greyhound.

How do you feel if you cross
a sheepdog with a melon?
Melon-Collie.

What do you get
if you cross a dog
with a frog?
**A dog that can
lick you from
across the room.**

What do you get if cross two young
dogs with a pair of headphones?
Hush puppies.

What do you get if you
cross a Cocker Spaniel,
a Poodle, and a rooster?
Cockerpoodledoo.

What do you get if you cross a
hunting dog with a telephone?
A Golden Receiver.

When does a dog go "moo?"
**When it is learning
a new language.**

What kind of dog
chases anything red?
A bull dog.

What do you get if you
cross a dog and a skunk?
Rid of the dog!

New Dog Breeds

- **A Blue Skye—*a dog with vision.***
  (A cross between a Kerry Blue Terrier
  and a Skye Terrier.)

- **A Peekasso—*an artistic dog.***
  (A cross between a Pekingnese and
  a Lhasa Apso.)

- **An Irish Springer—*a dog that's clean as a whistle.*** (A cross between an Irish Water Spaniel and an English Springer Spaniel.)

- **A Lab Coat Retriever— *a scientific dog.*** (A cross between a Labrador Retriever and a Curly Coated Retriever.)

- **A Newfound Asset Hound—**
  a dog that's good with money.
  (A cross between a Newfoundland and
  a Basset Hound.)

- **A Terribull—***a dog that behaves
  terribly.* (A cross
  between a Terrier
  and a Bulldog.)

- **A Blabador—*a dog that barks a lot.*** (A cross between a Bloodhound and a Labrador.)

- **A Commute—a dog that travels to school.** (A cross between a Collie and a Malamute.)

- **A Derriere—a dog that's true to the end.** (A cross between a Deerhound and a Terrier.)

91

How do you catch a monkey?
Hang from a tree and make a noise like a banana.

What kind of monkey flies to school?
A hot air baboon.

What is the best thing to do if you find a gorilla in your bed?
Sleep somewhere else.

What do you call an exploding monkey?
A ba-boom.

What do you get if you cross a cat and a gorilla?
An animal that puts you out at night.

What is a chimp's favorite snack?
Chocolate chimp cookies.

ooh
ooh
ooh

What do baby
apes sleep in?
Ape-ricots.

What do monkeys
eat for dessert?
Meringue-utans.

94

What's the first thing
an ape learns in school?
The ape b c's.

When do monkeys
fall from the sky?
During ape-ril showers.

What kind of cats like to go bowling?
Alley cats.

How does a lion greet the
other animals in the field?
"Pleased to eat you."

What is a French cat's favorite pudding?
Chocolate mousse.

What happened when
the lion ate the comedian?
He felt funny.

What do you get if you
cross a cat with a canary?
A peeping Tom.

What do you get if you
cross a cat with a tree?
A cat-a-logue.

What's the unluckiest
kind of cat to have?
A catastrophe.

What works in a circus,
walks a tightrope,
and has claws?
An acrocat.

There were four cats in a boat, and
one jumped out. How many were left?
None. They were all copy cats.

How do you spell mousetrap
in just three letters?
C-A-T.

What do you get if cross
a cat with a canary?
Shredded tweet.

Why is a frog luckier than a cat?
**Because a frog croaks all
the time but a cat only gets
to croak nine times.**

A Trunk Full of Laughs!

Why do elephants
scratch themselves?
**Because they're the only ones
who know where they itch.**

How does an elephant
get down from a tree?
**It sits on a leaf and
waits till autumn.**

Why did the elephant paint
itself with different colors?
**Because it wanted to hide
in the coloring box.**

How do you know that
peanuts are fattening?
**Have you ever seen
a skinny elephant?**

What's the difference
between an injured elephant
and bad weather?
**One roars with pain and
the other pours with rain.**

What's the difference between an elephant and a mail box?

I don't know.

Well, then I'm not going to ask you to mail my letters!

What's the difference between an elephant and a bad pupil?

One rarely bites and the other barely writes.

How to you tell the difference
between an elephant
and a mouse?

**Try picking
them up.**

Why do elephants
never forget?

**Because nobody
ever tells them anything.**

What's the difference between
an elephant and a piece of paper?
**You can't make a paper airplane
out of an elephant.**

What's the difference between
an elephant and a banana?
**Have you ever tried
to peel an elephant?**

What's the difference between
an African elephant and
an Indian elephant?
About 3,000 miles.

What's the difference between an elephant and a gooseberry?
A gooseberry is green.

Have you heard about the elephant that went on a crash diet?
It wrecked three cars, a bus, and two fire engines.

Why do elephants eat raw food?
Because they don't know how to cook.

Why did the elephant
eat the candle?
For light refreshment.

How can you tell if there is an
elephant in your dessert?
You get very lumpy ice cream.

What kind of
elephants live
in Antartica?
Cold ones.

How do you fit five
elephants into a car?
**Two in the front, two in
the back, and the other
in the glove compartment.**

How does an elephant
get out of a small car?
The same way that it got in.

Why do elephants have trunks?
**Because they would look
silly carrying suitcases.**

What to you get if you cross
a parrot with an elephant?
**An animal that tells you
everything that it remembers.**

What is a baby elephant
after it is five weeks old?
Six weeks old.

Police officer: One of your
elephants has been seen
chasing a man on a bicycle.
**Zoo keeper: Nonsense, none
of my elephants know how
to ride a bicycle.**

Why do the elephants
have short tails?
**Because they can't
remember long stories.**

How to you keep an
elephant in suspense?
I'll tell you tomorrow.

My elephant has no trunk.
How does it smell?
Terrible.

How do you hire an elephant?
Stand it on four bricks.

What is the easy way to
get a wild elephant?
Get a tame one and annoy it.

What did Tarzan say when he
saw the elephants coming?
"Here come the elephants."

Why is an elephant
braver than a hen?
**Because the elephant
isn't chicken.**

What is worse than
raining cats and dogs?
Raining elephants.

How are elephants and
hippopotamuses alike?
Neither can play basketball.

What did the baby elephant get
when the daddy elephant sneezed?
Out of the way!

How do you raise
a baby elephant?
With a fork lift.

Teacher: Where would you
find an elephant?
**Pupil: You don't have to find them.
They're too big to lose!**

What's the best way to see a charging herd of elephants?

On television.

Teacher: To which family does the elephant belong?

Pupil: I don't know; nobody that I know owns one.

Teacher: How do you spell elephant?

Pupil: E-l-l-e-e-f-a-n-t

Teacher: That's not how the dictionary spells it.

Pupil: You didn't ask me how the dictionary spells it!

Teacher: Name six wild animals.
Pupil: Four elephants and two lions.

Why did the elephant
have a lousy vacation?
The airline lost his trunk.

Why don't elephants
like to go swimming?
Because it's hard to
keep their trunks up.

How do you make an
elephant float?
**Add an elephant to two scoops of
vanilla ice cream and some milk.**

What do you get if you cross
a jaguar and an elephant?
A car with a big trunk.

What do you do when an
elephant stubs his toe?
Call a toe truck.

Why is an elephant so wrinkled?
**Because it's too big to fit
on an ironing board.**

Why does an elephant
wear sneakers?
So that it can sneak up on mice.

119

How do you get an
elephant to follow you?
Act like a nut.

What's grey and moves at
100 miles an hour?
A jet propelled elephant.

What's yellow on the outside
and grey on the inside?
An elephant disguised as a banana.

What's big, grey, and
flies straight up?
An elecopter.

What's grey, carries
a bunch of flowers,
and cheers you up
when your ill?
A get wellephant.

What's big and
grey and red?
A sunburned elephant.

What did the hotel manager
say to the elephant that
couldn't pay his bill?

"Pack your trunk and clear out."

What weighs four tons
and is bright red?

An elephant holding its breath.

What's grey and wrinkly and
jumps every 20 seconds?

An elephant with hiccups.

Why did the elephant
eat the candle?
It wanted a light snack.

What goes up slowly and
comes down quickly?
An elephant in an elevator.

What's as big as an elephant
but weighs nothing?
An elephant's shadow.

What do you get if you cross
an elephant and a kangaroo?
Big holes all over Australia.

Ding dong.
Who's there?
Albee.
Albee who?
**Albee outside
if you need me.**

Ding dong.
Who's there?
Albert.
Albert who?
Albert you don't know who this is.

Ding dong.
Who's there?
Justin.
Justin who?
Justin the neighborhood and thought I'd stop by.

Ding dong.
Who's there?
Oswald.
Oswald who?
Oswald my gum.

Ding dong.
Who's there?
Your mom.
Your mom who?
**You don't know
who your mom is?**

Ding dong.

Who's there?

Spell.

Spell who?

W-H-O.

Ding dong.
Who's there?
Tank.
Tank who?
Your welcome.

Ding dong.
Who's there?
Offer.
Offer who?
**Offer got my key,
let me in.**

Ding dong.
Who's there?
Ima.
Ima who?
**Ima coming in,
so open up.**

Ding dong.
Who's there?
Steel.
Steel who?
Steel waiting for you to open up.

Ding dong.
Who's there?
Keith.
Keith who?
**Keith me
thweet heart.**

Ding dong.

Who's there?

Golieth.

Golieth who?

**Golieth down,
you looketh tired.**

Ding dong.
Who's there?
Dewey.
Dewey who?
**Dewey have to listen
to all this dinging?**

Ding dong.
Who's there?
Ivana.
Ivana who?
Ivana be rich.

Ding dong.
Who's there?
Amahl.
Amahl who?
Amahl shook up.

Ding dong.
Who's there?
Anita.
Anita who?
**Anita come in
and use the bathroom.**

Ding dong.
Who's there?
Apple.
Apple who?
**Apple your hair if
you don't let me in.**

Ding dong.
Who's there?
Arch.
Arch who?
You catching a cold?

Ding dong.
Who's there?
Bacon.
Bacon who?
**Bacon a cake
for your birthday.**

Ding dong.
Who's there?
Boo.
Boo who?
Don't cry it's only a joke.

Ding dong.
Who's there?
Butter.
Butter who?
Butter bring an umbrella, it might rain.

Ding dong.
Who's there?
Cheese.
Cheese who?
Cheese a cute girl.

Ding dong.
Who's there?
Chicken.
Chicken who?
**Chicken the oven,
the cookies are
burning.**

147

Ding dong.
Who's there?
Thistle.
Thistle who?
Thistle have to hold you over until dinner's ready.

Ding dong.
Who's there?
Adolf.
Adolf who?
Adolph ball hit me in de mowf. Dat's why I dawk dis way.

Ding dong.
Who's there?
I love.
I love who?
**I don't know,
you tell me.**

Ding dong.

Who's there?

Police.

Police who?

Police stop telling these awful ding dong jokes.

Ding dong.
Who's there?
Mary Lee.
Mary Lee who?
**Mary Lee we
roll along.**

Ding dong.
Who's there?
Who.
Who, who?
**What are you,
some kind of owl?**

Ding dong.
Who's there?
Cow-go.
Cow-go Who?
No, cow go MOO...

Ding dong.
Who's there?
Moo.
Moo, who?
**Well, make
up your mind, are you
a cow or an owl?**

Ding dong.

Who's there?

Dwane.

Dwane who?

**Dwane the bathtub—
I'm dwowning.**

Knock knock.

Who's there?

A little girl.

A little girl who?

A little girl who can't reach the doorbell.

Ding dong.
Who's there?
Lettuce.
Lettuce who?
Lettuce in and you will find out.

Ding dong.
Who's there?
Ivan.
Ivan who?
**Ivan to suck
your blood.**

Ding dong.

Who's there?

Norma Lee.

Norma Lee who?

Norma Lee I don't go around ringing doorbells, but do you want to buy a set of encyclopedias?

Ding dong.
Who's there?
Wendy.
Wendy who?
**Wendy wind blows
de cradle will rock.**

Ding dong.
Who's there?
Theodore.
Theodore who?
**Theodore is stuck
and it won't close.**

Ding dong.
Who's there?
Sara.
Sara who?
**Sara doctor
in the house?**

Ding dong.

Who's there?

Yule.

Yule who?

Yule never know.

Ding dong.
Who's there?
Madam.
Madam who?
**Madam, my finger
is stuck in the door.**

Ding dong.

Who's there?

Water.

Water who?

Water you doing in my house?

Ding dong.
Who's there?
Isabelle.
Isabelle who?
**Isabelle necessary
on the door?**

Ding dong.
Who's there?
Dot.
Dot who?
**Dots for me to know,
and you to find out.**

Ding dong.
Who's there?
Pecan.
Pecan who?
**Pecan someone
your own size.**

Ding dong.
Who's there?
Annie.
Annie who?
**Annie thing you can
do, I can do better.**

Ding dong.
Who's there?
Danielle.
Danielle who?
Danielle, I can hear you.

Ding dong.

Who's there?

Yassine.

Yassine who?

Yassine a lost kitten wandering around here?

Ding dong.
Who's there?
Yassime.
Yassime who?
**Yassime a little
tired today.**

Ding dong.
Who's there?
Oliver.
Oliver who?
**Oliver across the
road from you.**

Ding Dong.
Who's there?
Anymore.
Anymore who?
**Anymore of
these jokes and
I'm outta here.**

Whad'ya call a monster that
was locked in the freezer?
A cool ghoul.

Whad'ya call artificial spaghetti?
Mockaroni.

Whad'ya call a flying skunk?
A smell-icopter.

Whad'ya call a snowman
with a suntan?
A puddle.

Whad'ya call shoes made
from banana skin?
Slippers.

Whad'ya call a chicken
that crosses the road
without looking both ways?
Dead.

Whad'ya call a blind dinosaur?
I-don't-think-he-saurus.

Whad'ya call 20 rabbits
moving backward?
A receding hare line.

Whad'ya call a country where
everyone has to drive a red car?
A red carnation.

Whad'ya call a frozen policeman?
A copsicle.

Whad'ya call a 10 foot tall monster?
Shorty.

Whad'ya call an elephant
at the North Pole?
Lost.

Whad'ya call a carousel
with no brakes?
**Merry-go-round, and round,
and round, and round.**

Whad'ya call
an arctic cow?
An Eskimoo.

Whad'ya call a pig that does karate?
A pork chop.

Whad'ya call a calf after
it's six months old?
Seven months old.

Whad'ya call a lazy kangaroo?
A pouch potato.

Whad'ya call it when
one cat sues another?
A clawsuit.

Whad'ya call a cat
with eight legs that
likes to swim?
An octopuss.

Whad'ya call a lion that has
eaten your mother's sister?
An aunt-eater.

Whad'ya call baby dogs that
come in from the snow?
Slush puppies.

Whad'ya call a black Eskimo dog?
A dusky Husky.

Whad'ya call a dog in the
middle of a muddy road?
A mutt in a rut.

Whad'ya call an
elephant that flies?
A jumbo jet.

Whad'ya call
a elephant that
never washes?
A smellyphant.

Whad'ya call an elephant
with a carrot in each ear?
**Anything you want—
he can't hear you.**

Whad'ya call a dismal dog?
A grey hound.

Whad'ya call a nutty
dog in Australia?
A dingo-ling.

Rib Ticklers!

How many morons does it take
to screw in a light bulb?
**Three...one to hold the bulb
and two to turn the chair.**

How do you confuse a moron?
**Put him in a round room and
tell him to sit in the corner.**

How can you tell when a moron
has been using the computer?
**There is white-out
all over the screen.**

What did the moron say
when he saw Cheerios?
"Oh look, donut seeds."

How do you keep
a moron in suspense?
I'll tell you tomorrow.

What has a lot of keys
but cannot open any doors?
A piano.

What has one horn and gives milk?
A milk truck.

What's gray, eats fish, and lives
in Washington, D.C.?
The presidential seal.

What did the rug
say to the floor?
**Don't move,
I've got you covered.**

What did the necktie say to the hat?
"You go on ahead. I'll hang around for a while."

Where do fortune tellers dance?
At the crystal ball.

What is big, red, furry
and knocks you over?
Tackle Me Elmo.

If a long dress is evening wear,
what is a suit of armor?
Silverware.

What bird can lift the most?
A crane.

What can you hold
without ever touching it?
A conversation.

What clothes does a house wear?
Address.

What country makes you shiver?
Chile.

What did one elevator
say to the other?
**"I think I'm coming
down with something."**

What did one magnet
say to the other?
"I find you very attractive."

What did the mother broom
say to the baby broom?
"It's time to go to sweep."

194

How do you make friends
with a computer?
Bit by bit.

Why is a
calendar so sad?
**Because its days
are numbered.**

What did one
arithmetic book
say to the other?
**"I've got a
lot of problems."**

What has two arms
but can't raise them?
A chair.

Why do ghosts like health food?
Because it's super natural.

What did one penny say
to the other penny?
We make perfect cents.

Why is a room full of married people empty? **Because there's not a single person in it.**

197

What did the alien
say to the plant?
**"Take me to
your weeder."**

What did one autumn
leaf say to another?
**"I'm falling
for you."**

How can your pocket be empty
and still have something in it?
When it has a hole in it.

Why did the baker rob the bank?
He needed the dough.

What did one vacuum
cleaner say to the other?
"Suck it up."

What do the moon and
false teeth have in common?
They both come out at night.

199

Why did the old man
put his car in the oven?
He wanted a hot rod.

Why did the
prisoner want to
get measles?
**So he could
break out.**

Why do roaches like to live in other people's homes?
Because they don't have to pay rent.

What word begins with e and has only one letter in it?
Envelope.

What figures do the most walking?
Roman numerals.

How many vampires does it
take to put in a lightbulb?
None, vampires like the dark.

What color do you paint
the sun and the wind?
The sun rose, and the wind blue.

Which brand of underwear
does King Tut like best?
Fruit of the Tomb.

What are the strongest
days of the week?
**Saturday and Sunday,
the rest are all week days.**

Which runs faster, hot or cold?
Hot, anyone can catch a cold.

Did you hear about the
depressed archeologist?
His life was in ruins.

What season is it when
you are on a trampoline?
Spring time.

What is black, white,
and red all over?
A panda with the measles.

What is green, purple
and 1,500 miles long?
The Grape Wall of China.

What is the most dangerous city?
Electricity.

What is very light, but can't
be held for long?
Your breath.

What is the richest kind of air?
Million-air.

When does Christmas come
before Thanksgiving?
In a dictionary.

When do cannibals
leave the table?
After everyone's eaten.

What word is always
pronounced wrong?
Wrong.

Who were the first people to invent
a plane that couldn't fly ?
The Wrong Brothers.

Do you want to hear
a construction joke?
Sorry, I'm still working on it.

What do you lose every
time you stand up?
Your lap.

Why did the man put
his money in the freezer?
He wanted cold hard cash.

Where do snowmen
keep their money?
In snow banks.

How can you double your money?
By folding it in half.

What did the water say to the boat?
Nothing, it just waved.

What did the ground
say to the earthquake?
"You crack me up."

How did the magician
cut the sea in half?
With a sea saw.

What letters are
not in the alphabet?
The ones in the mail.

Why was six afraid of seven?
Because seven eight nine.

What is the best day
to go to the beach?
Sunday, of course.

What bow can't be tied?
A rainbow.

What does a teddy bear
put in his house?
Fur-niture.

How do you fix
a car in Scotland?
With Scotch tape.

Where did the
computer go
to dance?
To a disc-o.

ooh
ooh
ooh

What has one head,
one foot, and four legs?
A bed.

What is the difference
between a school teacher
and a train?
**The teacher says,
"Spit out your gum,"
and the train says,
"Chew chew chew."**

Did you hear the joke
about the roof?
**Never mind,
it's over your head.**

How do you get rid of a boomerang?
Throw it down a one-way street.

What washes up on
very small beaches?
Microwaves.

What gets bigger and bigger as
you take more away from it?
A hole.

What goes through towns, up and
over hills, but doesn't move?
The road.

How do you make a bandstand?
Take away their chairs.

How do you start
a fire with two sticks?
**Make sure one of
the sticks is a match.**

What did the little mountain
say to the big mountain?
"Hi Cliff."

What do lawyers
wear to court?
Lawsuits.

Why couldn't the
pirate play cards?
**Because he was
sitting on the deck.**

Why did the traffic light turn red?
**You would too if you had
to change in the middle
of the street.**

What starts with a P, ends with
an E, and has a million letters in it?
Post Office.

What runs but can't walk?
The faucet.

Why didn't the hotdog
star in the movies?
The rolls weren't good enough.

What did the duck say
when it bought lipstick?
"Put it on my bill."

Why wouldn't they let the
butterfly into the dance?
Because it was a moth ball.

What did the tornado
say to the car?
"You wanna go for a spin?"

What do mermaids have on toast?
Mermerlade.

What kind of music do mummies like?
"Wrap" music.

What goes "Oh, Oh, Oh?"
Santa walking backward.

Why were the suspenders
sent to jail?
**They held up
a pair of trousers.**

What's smaller than
an ant's mouth?
An ant's dinner.

Why is it a bad idea to write
a letter on an empty stomach?
**Because it's much better
to write on paper.**

Did you hear the joke
about the jump rope?
No, I skipped it.

Why should you never
play games in the wild?
Because of all the cheetahs.

What's the hardest part
about sky diving?
The ground.

What kind of truck
do ballerinas drive?
Toe trucks.

What is a boxer's
favorite part of a joke?
The punch line.

Why were the police
at the baseball game?
**They heard someone
stole second base.**

What do you get when you cross
a baseball player with a boy scout?
**Someone who likes
to pitch tents.**

Why did the ballerina quit?
Because it was tu-tu hard.

Why did the boxer
wear gloves to bed?
**Because he wanted
to hit the sack.**

How do athletes stay
cool during a game?
They stand near the fans.

What game do people
play in the mall?
Price-tag.

Why did the tightrope
walker visit the bank?
**He wanted to
check his balance.**

If an athlete gets athlete's foot,
what does an astronaut get?
Missle toe.

What animal is best
at hitting a baseball?
A bat.

What baseball player
lives under a tree?
Babe Root.

Why was the
computer so
good at golf?
**Because it had
a hard drive.**

When is a boxer
like an astronomer?
When he sees stars.

What is a cheerleader's
favorite food?
Cheerios.

What is a cheerleader's
favorite drink?
Root beer.

What's a cheerleader's
favorite color?
Yeller.

What does baseball
have in common
with pancakes?
**They both rely
on the batter.**

229

Why shouldn't you tell
a joke while ice skating?
The ice might crack up.

Which athletes aren't
allowed to listen to music?
Those who've broken records.

Why can't a bicycle stand up?
Because it's two tired.

Why did the basketball
player go to jail?
Because he shot the ball.

Why did the coach go to the bank?
To get his quarter back.

What drink do boxers like?
Fruit punch.

What time of year do you
jump on a trampoline?
Spring time.

What does the winner
of a race lose?
Her breath.

What do you get when you
tie two bikes together?
Siamese Schwinns.

What is the funniest bike?
A Yamahahahahaha.

What's a golfer's favorite letter?
Tee.

What did the two strings
do in the race?
They tied.

What's a personal foul?
Your very own chicken.

What's the best smelling
position on a football team?
Right Guard.

What's the difference between
a dentist and a Yankees fan?
**One roots for the yanks and
the other yanks for the roots.**

What's the scariest
position on a
soccer team?
The ghoulie.

Which sport is
always in trouble?
Bad-minton.

Why are baseball
players so rich?
**Because they play
on diamonds.**

Why are most baseball
games held at night?
**Because the bats sleep
during the day.**

Why did Cinderella get
kicked off the soccer team?
**Because she ran away
from the ball.**

What do you say
to a chicken before
the big game?
"Break an egg."

What does a martial arts fan eat?
Kung food.

Why did the golfer wear
two pairs of pants?
In case he got a hole-in-one.

Why does it take longer to run from
second base to third base than it
takes to run from first to second?
**Because you have a short stop
between second and third.**

Why did the surfer
wear a baseball glove?
**Because he wanted
to catch a wave.**

Why do basketball
players love cookies?
Because they can dunk them.

Why does a wrestler bring
a key to the match?
To get out of a headlock.

Why don't grasshoppers
go to baseball games?
They prefer cricket.

What a Gag!

Why did the farmer
plant seeds in a pond?
He wanted to grow water-melons.

Who is Snow White's brother?
Egg White.
Get the yolk?

Why don't they serve
chocolate in prison?
Because it makes you break out.

Why do bananas put
on suntan lotion?
To keep from peeling.

Why did the man at the orange
juice factory lose his job?
He couldn't concentrate.

Where was the first donut made?
In Grease.

Why did the jelly roll?
Because it saw the apple turn over.

Where does a judge eat lunch?
At the food court.

What super hero lives in a pot?
Souperman.

Who serves ice cream faster
than a speeding bullet?
Scooperman.

What kind of garden
does a baker have?
A flour garden.

What did the police say
to the bad popsicle?
"Freeze."

What is Harry Potter's
favorite cereal?
Lucky Charms.

Why did the apple
go out with a fig?
Because it couldn't find a date.

Why were the orange
and the apple all alone?
Because the banana split.

Why did the banana peel?
It didn't have any suntan lotion on.

Why did the orange stop rolling?
Because it was out of juice.

Have you heard the
joke about the butter?
I won't tell.
You might spread it.

How can you drop an egg
three feet and not break it?
Drop it four feet—for the first
three feet it won't break.

What do bananas do
best in gymnastics?
The splits.

How can you get breakfast in bed?
Sleep in the kitchen.

What do you call 10,000
strawberries squeezing
through a doorway?
Strawberry jam.

What is the fruitiest lesson?
History, because it's full of dates.

ooh
ooh
ooh

What key do you use
to open a banana?
A monkey.

What do you get when
two peas fight?
Black-eyed peas.

What is the most dangerous
veggie to have on a boat?
A leek.

What is the pickle
capital of the world?
Dill-adelphia.

What is the strongest
vegetable in the world?
Muscle sprout.

What kind of beans never
grow in a garden?
Jelly beans.

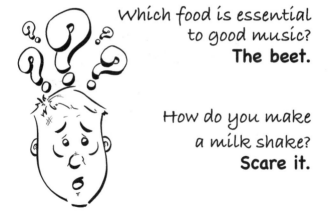

Which food is essential
to good music?
The beet.

How do you make
a milk shake?
Scare it.

What's a tree's favorite drink?
Root beer.

Which is the funniest soda?
Joke-a-cola.

Do you know the watermelon joke?
It's pit-a-ful.

How do you make
a strawberry shake?
Put it in the refrigerator.

How many bananas does it
take to screw in a lightbulb?
A bunch.

How many lemons
grow on a lemon tree?
All of them.

If you hold nine oranges in
one hand and ten lemons in the
other, what do you have?
Really big hands.

What are strawberries
when they are sad?
Blueberries.

What are twins' favorite fruits?
Pears.

What did the raspberry
say to the blueberry?
"I love you berry, berry much."

What did the two melons say
when they got engaged?
"Too bad we cantaloupe."

In which country do people's tummies rumble most?
Hungary.

Is your refrigerator running?
It is? Well, you'd better go and catch it.

What are two things you cannot have for lunch?
Breakfast and dinner.

What bird is good
at making bread?
A dough dough.

What candy is never on time?
Choco-late.

What country did
candy come from?
Sweeten.

What did one plate say
to the other plate?
Food's on me tonight.

What did one potato chip
say to the other chip?
"Want to go for a dip?"

What did the donut say
about the weather forecast?
**"Tonight, there will be
lots of sprinkles."**

What did the salt say to the pepper?
"Hey, what's shaking?"

What did the vanilla
ice cream say to the
chocolate ice cream?
**"Have I melt
you before?"**

What do cattle order
in Italian restaurants?
Cow-zones.

What do elves make
sandwiches with?
Shortbread.

What do you call
a train loaded with taffy?
A chew chew train.

What do you call cheese
that you don't own?
Nacho cheese.

What do you get if you
cross a snake with a pie?
A pie-thon.

What do you get when you
cross a camera and a mouse?
Cheese.

What do you get when you cross
a cheetah and a hamburger?
Fast food.

What food stays hot
no matter how cold it is?
A pepper.

What is a geologist's
favorite ice cream flavor?
Rocky Road.

What is a pie's favorite sport?
Pie Kwan Do.

What is a rock's favorite cereal?
Cocoa Pebbles.

What is the best thing
to put in a pie?
Your teeth.

When do you stop on
green and go on red?
When you eat a watermelon.

When is the moon not hungry?
When it is full.

Where did the hamburger
take his date?
To the meat ball.

Where do smart butters go?
On the honor roll.

Who writes nursery rhymes
and squeezes oranges?
Mother Juice.

Why are cooks so cruel?
**Because they beat the
eggs and whip the cream.**

Why did the boy put
sugar under his pillow?
So he would have sweet dreams.

Why did the
donut go to
the dentist?
**To get a
chocolate filling.**

Why is honey so scarce in Boston?
**Because there is only one
B in Boston.**

Why is Swiss cheese
served at church?
Because it's holey.

What did Baby Corn
say to Mama Corn?
"Where's Pop Corn?"

What did Popeye say to the potato?
"I yam what I yam."

What did the boy lettuce
say to the girl lettuce?
"Lettuce be friends."

What kind of fruit do
trees like the most?
Pine-apples.

What kind of jam would
you not want to eat?
A traffic jam.

What kind of
security systems
do fast food
places have?
Burger alarms.

What kind of soup
never gets hot?
Chilli soup.

What's the difference between
bread and the sun?
**The sun rises in the East, and
bread rises from the yeast.**

How do you cook toast
in the jungle?
Put it under a gorilla.

How do you fix a broken pizza?
Tomato paste.

How do you make a cream puff?
Chase it around the block.

How do you make a hot dog stand?
Take away its chair.

270

How do you make a walnut laugh?
Crack it up.

How do you make an egg roll?
Push it.

How do you make gold soup?
Add 14 carrots.

How do you start your
day with a smile?
By eating grin-ola for breakfast.

How does a turkey eat its food?
It gobbles it up.

What do astronauts eat for dinner?
Launch meat.

Why did the tomato blush?
Because it saw the salad dressing.

What do you call
a nervous celery stalk?
An edgy veggie.

Why can't bananas
grow any longer?
**Because they're
long enough already.**

What did the grape do
when it got stepped on?
It let out a little wine.

Why did the cookie
go to the hospital?
Because it felt crummy.

How do you know carrots
are good for your eyes?
**Because you never see
rabbits wearing glasses.**

274

Why did the boy eat his homework?
**Because his teacher said
it was a piece of cake.**

Why did the jelly wobble?
Because it saw the milk shake.

What happens if you
eat yeast and shoe polish?
Every morning you'll rise and shine.

Why was the guy looking
for the food on his friend?
Because his friend said it's on me.

Why did Tony go out
with a prune?
**Because he couldn't
find a date.**

What do bees chew?
Bumble gum.

What bee is good for your health?
Vitamin bee.

What is a dog's favorite food?
Anything that is on your plate.

What do you do if your
dog eats your pen?
Use a pencil instead.

What happened to the dog
that ate nothing but garlic?
**Its bark was much
worse than its bite.**

What happens to a dog that keeps
eating bites off of the table?
It gets splinters in its mouth.

What did the hungry Dalmatian
say when it had a meal?
"That hit the spots."

Silly States

What states needs a tissue?
"Mass-a-choooo-setts."

What state is a spilled color?
"Loose-sienna."

What did "Missis sip?"
She sipped a Minnesoda.

How did "Flora die?"
She died in Missouri.

What did "Tenna see?"
The same thing Arkansas.

What did "Dela wear?"
She wore her New Jersey.

What else did "Dela wear?"
I don't know, Alaska.

What is the bandaid state?
"Connect-a-cut."

What state is high in the middle
and round on both ends?
Ohio (look at the letters).

What is the happiest state?
"Merryland."

What state is easiest to drive in?
"Road Island."

How do you know the sun came
up today?
Utah it!

What state is inside another state?
Kansas is in Arkansas.

What state is full of color?
"Color-ado."

What state weighs the most?
Washington.

What state is on a horse?
"Mane."

What state needs to be sharpened?
"Pencil-vania."

What do you call a hippie's wife?
Mississippi.

Clown School!

Ooh
Ooh
Ooh

Teacher: Johnny, give me
a sentence starting with "I."
Johnny: I is...
Teacher: No, Johnny.
Always say, "I am."
**Johnny: All right... "I am the
ninth letter of the alphabet."**

**Child: Dad, can you
write in the dark?**
Father: I think so. What do
you want me to write?
**Child: Your name on
this report card.**

Teacher: What's 2 plus 2?
Pupil: 4.
Teacher: That's good.
Pupil: Good? That's perfect!

Teacher: How much is half of 8?
Pupil: Up and down or across?
Teacher: What do you mean?
**Pupil: Well, up and down makes a 3
or across the middle leaves a 0.**

Why did the teacher put the lights on?
Because the class was so dim.

Teacher: Johnny, why do you always get so dirty?
Pupil: Well, I'm a lot closer to the ground then you are.

Teacher: Suzy, how do you spell "crocodile?"
Suzy: K-R-O-K-O-D-A-I-L.
Teacher: No, that's wrong.
Suzy: Maybe it's wrong, but you ask me how I spell it.

What is a forum?
Two-um plus two-um.

Great news—Teacher says we have a
test today, come rain or shine.
So, what's so great about that?
It's snowing outside!

What would you get if you crossed a
vampire and a teacher?
Lots of blood tests.

Where did all the cuts
and blood come from?
The school went on a trip.

What's the worst thing you're likely
to find in the school cafeteria?
The food.

What kind of food
do math teachers eat?
Square meals.

Why don't you see giraffes
in elementary school?
Because they're all in high school.

What room can
a student never enter?
A mushroom.

Teacher: Where is your homework?
**Pupil: Our puppy potty-trained
on it.**

If there are ten cats in a boat and one jumps out, how many are left?
None, they were all copycats.

Teacher: Now class, whatever I ask, I want you to all answer all at once. How much six plus four?
Class: All at once!

Teacher: Class, we will have only half a day of school this morning.

Class: Hooray!

Teacher: We will have the other half this afternoon.

Teacher: That's quite a cough you have there, what are you taking for it?

Pupil: I don't know teacher. What will you give me?

Teacher: You aren't paying attention to me. Are you having trouble hearing?

Pupil: No, teacher I'm having trouble listening.

Teacher: What are the Great Plains?
Pupil: 747, Concorde, and F-16.

Son: I can't go to school today.
Father: Why not?
Son: I don't feel well.
Father: Where don't you feel well?
Son: In school.

**I failed every subject
except for algebra.**
How did you keep from failing that?
I didn't take algebra.

Teacher: Are you good at math?
Pupil: Yes and no.
Teacher: What do you mean?
Pupil: Yes, I'm no good at math.

What are the small rivers that run into the Nile?
The juve-niles.

**Pupil (on phone): My son has
a bad cold and won't be able
to go to school today.**

School secretary: Who is this?

Pupil: This is my father speaking.

297

Pupil: My teacher was mad
at me because I didn't know
where the Rockies were.
**Mother: Well next time remember
where you put things.**

Mother: What was the first
thing you learned in class?
**Daughter: How to talk
without moving my lips.**

Teacher: What's big and yellow
and comes in the morning
to brighten a mother's day?
Pupil: The school bus.

298

Teacher: You missed school
    yesterday didn't you?
Pupil: Not very much.

Teacher: Where is your homework?
    **Pupil: I left it in my shirt,
        and my mother put it
        in the washing machine.**

299

Hilareous History!

300

When crossing the Delaware River, why did George Washington stand up in the boat?
He was afraid that if he sat down, someone would give him an oar to row.

What did they do at the Boston Tea Party?
I don't know, I wasn't invited.

What did they wear at the Boston Tea Party?
T-shirts.

Teacher: Why does the Statue of
Liberty stand in New York harbor?
Pupil: Because it can't sit down.

What was Camelot?
**A place where people
parked their camels.**

Where did the pilgrims land
when they came to America?
On their feet.

What did George Washington, Abraham Lincoln, and Christopher Columbus all have in common?

They were all born on holidays.

303

Teacher: George, go to the map and find North America.

George: Here it is.

Teacher: Correct.
Now, Johnny, can you tell us who discovered America?

Johnny: George.

What does the 1286BC inscribed on the mummy's tomb mean?

It's the license plate of the car that ran him over.

304

Who succeeded the first
president of the USA?
The second one.

Why does history keep
repeating itself?
**Because we weren't
listening the first time.**

Why were the early days of
history called the dark ages?
**Because there were
so many knights.**

How did Columbus's men
sleep on their ships?
With their eyes shut.

What was the greatest
accomplishment of
the Early Romans?
Speaking Latin.

Why did Robin Hood
only rob the rich?
**Because the poor didn't have
anything worth stealing.**

When did Caesar reign?
I didn't know he reigned.
Of course he did, didn't
they hail him?

Why was George Washington
buried at Mount Vernon?
Because he was dead.

Where did knights
learn to kill dragons?
At knight school.

307

Why did the pioneers cross the country in covered wagons?
Because they didn't want to wait 40 years for a train.

Why did the Romans build straight roads?
So their soldiers didn't go around the bend.

When a knight in armor was killed in battle, what sign did they put on his grave?
Rust in peace.

Do you know the 20th president of the United States?
No, we were never introduced.

My teacher reminds me of history.
She's always repeating herself.

Teacher: What can you tell me about the Dead Sea?

Pupil: Dead? I didn't even know it was sick.

What did Napoleon become when he was 41 years old?

A year older on his birthday.

Why can't The Invisible Man pass school?

The teacher always marks him absent.

Why did the teacher
marry the janitor?
**Because he swept
her off her feet.**

Teacher: Where is your homework?
**Pupil: I didn't do it because I
didn't want to add to your
already heavy workload.**

Teacher: Where is your homework?
Pupil: My little sister ate it.

Teacher: Where is your homework?
**Pupil: Some aliens from outer space
borrowed it so they could study
how the human brain worked.**

Teacher: Why were you late?

Pupil: Sorry, teacher, I overslept.

**Teacher: It's three in
the afternoon.**

Teacher: Where is your homework?

**Pupil: I loaned it to a friend,
but he suddenly moved away.**

Teacher: Where is your homework?
Pupil: Our furnace stopped working, and we had to burn it to stop ourselves from freezing.

Mother: What did you learn in school today?
Son: How to write.
Mother: What did you write?
Son: I don't know, they haven't taught us how to read yet.

Teacher: Where is the
English Channel?
**Pupil: I don't know,
my TV doesn't pick it up.**

Teacher: This is the third time I've had to discipline you this week! What have you got to say about that?

Pupil: Thank goodness it's Friday.

Teacher: Didn't you hear me call you?

Pupil: Yes, but you said not to talk back.

What tables don't you have to learn?

Dinner tables.

Why was the principal worried?
Because there were too many rulers in school.

Why did the teacher wear sunglasses?
Because his class was so bright.

What is a teacher's three favorite words?
June, July, and August.

1st Roman Soldier: What is the time?
2nd Roman Soldier: XX past VII.

Teacher: What family does
the octopus belong to?
Pupil: Nobody I know.

What's yellow, has wheels,
and lies on its back?
A dead school bus.

How do bees get to school?
By school buzz.

Teacher: I hope I didn't see you
looking at Fred's test paper.
**Pupil: I hope you
didn't see me either.**

Teacher: You copied from Fred's test didn't you?

Pupil: How did you know?

Teacher: Fred's test says "I don't know" and your test says, "Me, neither."

Teacher, I can't solve this problem.

Any 5-year-old should be able to solve this one.

No wonder I can't do it! I'm nearly 10.

Why did the girl turn
in her math book?
It had too many problems.

Why was the student's
report card all wet?
Because it was below C (sea) level.

Teacher: Why can't you ever
answer any of my questions?
**Pupil: Well, if I could, there
wouldn't be much point in
me being here.**

What did the computer
do at lunchtime?
Had a byte.

Dad, can you help me find the
lowest common denominator
in this problem please?
**Don't tell me that they haven't
found it yet, I remember looking
for it when I was a boy.**

Mother: Why did you just swallow the money I gave you?

Son: Well you did say it was my lunch money.

What's a mushroom?

The place they store the school food.

Teacher: Did your parents help you with these homework problems?

Pupil: No, I got them all wrong by myself.

Teacher: I said to draw a cow eating some grass—but you've only drawn the cow.

Pupil: Yes, the cow ate all the grass.

Father: How were
the test questions?

Son: Easy.

Father: Then why do
you look so unhappy?

**Son: The questions didn't give me
any trouble, just the answers.**

What are you going to be
when you get out of school?

Old.

What did you learn
in school today?
**Not enough, I have
to go back tomorrow.**

Mother: How was your
first day at school?
**Son: It was all right except for
some man called "Teacher" who
kept spoiling all our fun.**

I'm not going back
to school ever again.
Why not?
The teacher doesn't know a thing,
all she does is ask questions.

Pupil: I don't think I deserved
a zero on this test.
Teacher: I agree, but that's the
lowest mark I could give you.

Father: You were absent
on the day of the test?
**Son: No, but the boy who
sits next to me was.**

"It's clear," said the teacher,
"that you haven't studied your
geography. What's your excuse?"
**"Well, my dad says the world is
changing every day. So I decided
to wait until it settles down."**

Teacher: Where is your homework?
**Pupil: I put it in a safe, but
lost the combination.**

Are you in the top
half of your class?
**No, I'm one of
the students who
make the top
half possible.**

Art teacher: The picture
of the horse is good, but
where is the wagon?
Pupil: The horse will draw it.

Teacher: Why are you picking
your nose in class?
**Pupil: My mother won't
let me do it at home.**

Teacher: How can you prevent
diseases caused by biting insects?
Pupil: Don't bite any.

Teacher: What do you call a person who keeps on talking when people are no longer interested?

Pupil: A teacher.

Teacher: Johnny, your composition on "My Dog" is exactly the same as your brother's. Did you copy his?

Johnny: No, teacher, it's the same dog.

Teacher: What a pair of strange socks you are wearing. One is green, and one is blue with red spots.
Pupil: Yes it's really strange. I've got another pair of the same at home.

When was The Great Depression?
Last week, when I got my report card.

Teacher: Why are you reading the last pages of your history book first?

Pupil: I want to know how it ends.

Why did George Washington
chop down the cherry tree?
I'm stumped.

Why can't you send letters
to Washington anymore?
Because he died a long time ago.

I'm learning ancient history.
**So am I, let's go for a walk
and talk over old times.**

Abraham Lincoln had a very
hard childhood, he had to walk
7 miles to school every day.
**Well, he should have got up
earlier and caught the school
bus like everyone else.**

What do history teachers make
when they want to get together?
Dates.

What do they talk about?
The good old days.

Why did George Washington sleep standing up?
Because he couldn't lie.

Fun with Words!

Only in the English language...
**Can you park on driveways
and drive on parkways.**

Only in the English language...
**Can a "slim chance" and a "fat
chance" be the same thing.**

Only in the English language...
**Can a "wise man" and a
"wise guy" be opposites.**

Only in the English language...
**Can "overlook" and
"oversee" be opposites.**

Only in the English language...
**Does "quite a lot" and "quite a
few" mean the same thing.**

Only in the English language...
**Can your house go up and
down at the same time
(when it's burning).**

Only in the English language...
Can you fill in a form by filling it out.

Only in the English language...
Can stars be visible when they're out and lights be invisible when they're out.

Only in the English language...
Do you recite at a play and play at a recital.

Only in the English language ...
**Do you ship by truck and
send cargo by ship.**

Only in the English language...
Will teachers have taught, but preachers won't have praught.

Only in the English language...
Do vegetarians eat vegetables, but humanitarians don't eat humans.

Only in the English language...
Can an alarm clock go off by going on.

Only in the English language...
**Is there no egg in eggplant, no
ham in hamburger, and no pine
(or apple) in pineapple.**

343

What Did You Just Say?

Mondegreens are misheard words and song lyrics.

Actual lyric: More than a woman.
(by the Bee Gees)
What was heard: Four-legged woman.

Actual lyric: Big girls don't cry.
(by The Four Seasons)
What was heard: Big girl, small fry.

Actual lyric: You wore a shirt of violent green.
(by R.E.M.)
What was heard: You wore a skirt made of cream cheese.

Actual lyric: Big old jet airliner.
(by the Steve Miller Band)
What was heard: Big ole' Jed had a light on.

Actual lyric: Caribbean Queen, now we're sharing the same dreams.
(by Billy Ocean)
What was heard: Carryin' beans, now we're sharin' the same jeans.

Actual lyric: Unchain my heart.
(by Ray Charles)
What was heard: Come shave
my heart.

**Actual lyric: Dirty deeds and
they're done dirt cheap.**
(by ACDC)
What was heard: Dirty deeds
and the thunder chiefs.

Actual lyric: Don't stand so close to me.
(by The Police)
What was heard: Ghost man so close to me.

Actual lyric: I can't fight this feeling anymore.
(by REO Speedwagon)
What was heard: I can't climb this ceiling any more.

Actual lyric: Stayin' alive, stayin' alive.
(by the Bee Gees)
What was heard: I, I, I, I sing in the light, sing in the light.

Actual lyric: Taking care of business.
(by Bachman-Turner Overdrive)
What was heard: Baking carrot biscuits.

Actual lyric: A new religion that'll bring you to your knees, black velvet if you please.
(by Allanah Myles)
What was heard: A new religion that'll bring you to your knees, like Velveeta Cheese

Actual lyric: 'Scuse me, while I kiss the sky.
(by Jimi Hendrix)
What was heard: 'Scuse me while I kiss this guy.

Actual lyric: She's got a ticket to ride.
(by the Beatles)
What was heard: She's got a chicken to ride.

Actual lyric: Sugar Pie, Honey Bunch.
(by the Four Tops)
What was heard: Sugar fried honey butt.

Actual lyric: Then I saw her face, now I'm a believer.
(by *The Monkees*)
What was heard: Then I saw her face, now I'm gonna leave her.

Actual lyric: You may be right, I may be crazy.
(by *Billy Joel*)
What was heard: You made the rice, I made the gravy.

Actual lyric: I'm not the cat I used to be; I've got a kid, I'm 33, baby. (by The Pretenders)

What was heard: I'm not the cat I used to be; I've got a can of 33 babies...

353

Say That Again?

Redundancies are excessive word usage in writing and speaking.

"There was no advanced warning that the storm was coming."

Warnings always come in advance.

"Let's all meet together at the playground."

"Meeting" means gathering together.

"This puts me in a difficult dilemma."

Dilemmas are always difficult.

"A baby boy was born."

Of course it was a baby if it was just born.

"I wrote an autobiography of my life."

An autobiography is the story of someone's life.

357

"I commute back and forth to school on the bus."

Commuting means traveling back and forth.

"I counted each and every pencil in the box."

Doesn't "every" include "each"?

"Let's work in that empty space over there."

Isn't space already empty?

"The library had free gifts on Saturday."

Since when do you pay for gifts?

359

"Her pet frog was green in color."

In what other way would it be green?

"Never, at any time, should students enter the boiler room."

Doesn't "never" include "at any time?"

"I wonder if that pair of twins is fraternal or identical."

Are you talking about 4 people? Twins are already a pair.

"My past experiences have always been good with that teacher."

Your experiences are already in the past.

"Watch out for snakes with poisonous venom."

Venom is poisonous.

"My regular routine includes brushing my teeth."

Routines are already regular.

364

Look Both Ways!

Palindromes: Words or phrases
that can be read the same
in both directions.

- **Rats live on no evil star.**

- **Go hang a salami; I'm a lasagna hog.**

- **Dennis sinned.**

- **Never odd or even.**

- **Madam, I'm Adam.**

Fowl Play

Why did the birdie go to the hospital?
To get tweetment.

What is the opposite of
cock-a doodle-doo?
Cock-a-doodle-don't.

Why did the owl, owl?
**Because the woodpecker
would peck 'er.**

Why do seagulls fly over the sea?
Because if they flew over the bay, they would be bagels.

What do you get if you cross
a duck with a firework?
A firequaker.

If a rooster laid a brown egg
and a white egg, what kind
of chicks would hatch?
None. Roosters don't lay eggs.

Why are birds poor?
**Because money doesn't
grow on trees.**

371

What is green and pecks on trees?
Woody Wood Pickle.

What is a parrot's
favorite game?
Hide and Speak.

What is the
definition of Robin?
A bird that steals.

What's another name
for a clever duck?
A wise quacker.

Which bird is always out of breath?
A puffin.

What is a duck's favorite TV show?
The feather forecast.

374

What do you get if you
cross a parrot with a shark?
A bird that will talk your ear off.

What do you call a crate of ducks?
A box of quackers.

Where do birds invest their money?
In the stork market.

What do you get if you cross
a parrot with a woodpecker?
A bird that talks in Morse code.

What do you call a woodpecker
with no beak?
A headbanger.

What birds spend all their
time on their knees?
Birds of prey.

What did they call the canary
that flew into the pastry dish?
Tweetie Pie.

What kind of birds do you
usually find locked up?
Jail-birds.

What do you call a rooster
that wakes you up at the
same time every morning?
An alarm cluck.

377

What do you get if you cross
a chicken with a bell?
**A bird that has to
wring its own neck.**

Why did the dirty chicken
cross the road?
For some fowl purpose.

How do chickens dance?
Chick to chick.

379

Why did the Roman chicken
cross the road?
**Because it was afraid
someone would Caesar.**

Why did the chewing
gum cross the road?
**Because it was stuck
to the chicken.**

Why did the chicken
end up in the soup?
Because it ran out of cluck.

What do chickens grow on?
Eggplants.

What happens when
a hen eats gunpowder?
She lays hand gren-eggs.

Why did the chicken cross the "net?"
**It wanted to get to
the other site.**

Why did the chicken cross
the road half way?
He wanted to lay it on the line.

What does an alarm cluck say?
"Tick-tock-a-doodle-doo."

Why does a chicken
coop have two doors?
**Because if it had four doors, it
would be a chicken sedan.**

Why did the turkey cross the road?
To prove it wasn't chicken.

Why did the rooster cross the road?
To cockadoodle dooo something.

Why did the chick disappoint
his mother?
**He wasn't what he
was cracked up to be.**

Why did the chicken cross
the road, roll in the mud,
and cross the road again?
**Because he was a dirty
double-crosser.**

What goes peck, peck, peck, boom?
A chicken in a mine field.

Which came first, the
chicken or the egg?
Neither, the rooster.

Why did the elephant
cross the road?
**To pick up the
squashed chicken.**

What do you call a chicken that crosses the road without looking both ways?
Dead.

What was the farmer doing on the other side of the road?
Catching all the chickens that crossed the road.

Why did the duck cross the road?
Because the chicken retired and moved to Florida.

Did you hear the story about the peacock who crossed the road?
It is really a colorful tail...

What goes "peck, bang, peck, bang, peck, bang!"
A bunch of chickens in a field full of balloons.

What do you get if you cross a chicken with a cement mixer?
A brick-layer.

387

What kind of eggs does
a wicked chicken lay?
Deviled eggs.

Doctor, my grandmother's suffering from Deja Vu.
Didn't I see her yesterday?

Doctor, I feel like a spoon.
Well sit still and don't stir.

Doctor, my cousin said he feels like a pack of cards.
Tell him I'll deal with him later.

390

Doctor, my sister needs
a second opinion.
**Of course, tell her to
come back tomorrow.**

Doctor, I keep thinking I'm invisible.
Who said that?

Doctor, I think I need glasses.
**You certainly do, sir,
this is a pizza shop.**

391

Doctor, I think I'm a bell.
Give me a ring tomorrow.

Doctor: You need new glasses
Patient: How do you know?
I haven't told you what's
wrong with me yet.
**Doctor: I could tell as
soon as you walked in
through the window.**

393

Doctor, my father thinks I'm a snail.
**Don't worry we'll soon
have you out of your shell.**

**Doctor, I keep
seeing double.**
Please sit
on the couch.
Which one?

Doctor: You seem to be in excellent health. Your pulse is as regular as clockwork.

Patient: That's because you've got your hand on my watch.

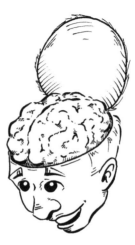

Doctor, what did the x-ray of my brother's head show? **Absolutely nothing.**

What Does That Mean?

Artery: The study of paintings

Benign: What you'll be after you're eight

Bacteria: Back door to the cafeteria

CAT scan: Searching for kitty

Coma: A punctuation mark

Hangnail: What you hang your coat on

Medical staff:
A doctor's cane

Outpatient: A person who has fainted

Recovery room: Place to do upholstery

Seizure: Roman emperor

Tablet: A small table

Terminal illness: Getting sick at the airport

Tumor: More than one

Urine: Opposite of you're out

400